KEEPING PEACE

REFLECTIONS ON LIFE, LEGACY, COMMITMENT AND STRUGGLE

CORNEL WEST   MICHAEL PFLEGER   HAKI R. MADHUBUTI

T0198469

Other titles by Lasana Kazembe

Not Our President: New Directions from the Pushed Out, the Others, the Clear Majority in Trump's Stolen America (Co-editor)

Write to Be: Poetry by Stateville Writers (Editor)

Nappyheaded Blackgirls: New Aesthetic, A

KEEPING PEACE

REFLECTIONS ON LIFE, LEGACY, COMMITMENT AND STRUGGLE

EDITED BY

LASANA KAZEMBE

FOREWORD BY

MICHAEL SIMANGA

Third World Press Foundation
Chicago

Third World Press Foundation
Publishers since 1967
Chicago

Third World Press Foundation
P.O. Box 19730
Chicago, IL 60619

First Edition
Printed in the United States of America
20 19 18 17 6 5 4 3 2 1

Library of Congress Control Number: 2017955543

Edited by Lasana D. Kazembe, PhD
Photography and images courtesy of Raynard Graves.

ISBN: 9780883784013

Publishing Black Writers *Fearlessly* for Fifty Years!
(1967-2017)

"There are days, this is one of them, when you wonder what your role is in this country and what your future is in it. How precisely you're going to reconcile yourself to your situation here and how you are going to communicate to the vast, heedless, unthinking, cruel white majority that you are here. And to be here means that you can't be anywhere else. I'm terrified at the moral apathy – the death of the heart – which is happening in my country. These people have deluded themselves for so long that they really don't think I'm human. I base this on their conduct. Not on what they say. And this means that they have become in themselves moral monsters. That's a terrible indictment, but I mean every word I say."

James Baldwin
PBS interview with Dr. Kenneth Clarke, 1963

l to r: Fr. Michael Pfleger, Lasana Kazembe, Cornel West, Haki R. Madhubuti

CONTENTS

Foreword

A Poet, a Preacher, and a Philospher...

...sit down to talk after greeting each other with warm laughter and the easy telling of quick stories from the last time they'd been together. There is genuine joy in the tones that emerge in their speech as they relax in the presence of each other's work and legacy. The commonality and differences in the paths they've walked and the ideas they've promulgated adds a respectful tension necessary for high-level exchange and learning. Knowledge of history suggests smiles are imminent from knowing that they are again in the company of those who have not only charged into uncounted battles for human rights and justice, it is their life commitment and practice. The deep and mutual respect is evident amongst these old friends who have been battle-tested and sometimes betrayed. Their ideas and work have expanded in understand and delivery. They have been criticized and often misunderstood and yet, they stood, and are still standing, in the growing storm we face today.

No longer young men, the poet, the preacher and the philosopher move slower but more effectively as the wisdom of decades makes the moves deceptively potent like Tai-Chi. Smooth, slow, focus on breath and execution, but still a deadly martial arts capable of taking down an aggressor moving to do harm to their people. There is still some thunder in their steps and because they are inspired by the uprising of the new the now generation, these veterans only walk heavy when needed. There is still the unmistakable and undeniable lightning in their voices. When they speak, you can hear lives of intense study to answer questions why, and strategy how, and lessons after and inspiration from their people and the experience of the world, our world the one we fight for, the world where there is justice for all of humanity.

The poet, Haki Madhubuti, the preacher, Father Michael Pfleger, and the philosopher, Cornel West came into and made a commitment to their work from varied experiences. Madhubuti grew up a brilliant Black boy who loved to read and lived in poverty of things but filled with the rich historical spirit of Black people determined to be free. He became a poet, one of the principal architects of the Black Arts Movement, a scholar, educator and the founder and publisher of Third World Press/Third World Press Foundation. Michael Pfleger was a rebellious teenager from a middle-class family in a White enclave of Chicago. He questioned the efficacy of racism while being pulled toward answers by the gravitational force of Dr. Martin Luther King's ideas and leadership. He saw the church of his faith as an institution that could affect change, became a priest and worked for social, economic and political justice in Chicago's Black south side. Cornel West grew up in a Black middle class family, went to Ivy League schools and became one of the foremost intellectuals of these times. He chose not to live a safe academic life. Instead he used his position as a public intellectual to challenge the structures and people responsible for the oppressive systems and practices that plague this country.

After decades of extraordinary dedication and work, scars zig-zag across their memories. They carry not quite healed wounds to their souls from the unending fight for justice. Their irrepressible spirit is draped across their shoulders like garments soaked in what the historian Vincent Harding called, *"our river of history."* Stories are tattooed on their tongues forming maps to the past and the places they fought battles for ideas like justice, liberation, freedom and peace.

They are brothers convened for a conversation and a moment to commune. The open wounds confirm their kinship even if it is not readily apparent they are brothers when viewed through the funhouse mirrors lining the halls of American democracy. We've looked at ourselves and each other through those mirrors for so long we don't know what we really look like to ourselves or each other. These men know what they look like and they see each other and they see us and smile because our collective scars and stories, our determination to build a world worthy of our lives is beautiful to them.

We knew Haki Madhubuti first as a poet in the 1960s because he spoke to and for us, Black people seeking liberation after the defeat and dismantling of Jim Crow. Black Power came roaring out of his verses. His poems, beacons of truth and light beaming into our eyes so that our voice could soar from the deepest spaces of the memories of our humanity. Those poems became tools, weapons to construct the new life we needed and to fight those who charged at us intent on dragging us back to the old life they wanted for us. His poems called forth a giant gathering of those who came before and those here now carrying all those rhythms from all those drums and all those harmonies from all those songs and chants and prayers over all those centuries, from all those fields on fire in the sun and all those endless miles of cold concrete and from all those marching feet and hands building, holding on and fighting.

If Haki had *only* been a poet it would have been enough for us. But he chose to do more, to make a life-long commitment to build critical education and political institutions to stabilize an often unstable movement in the ebb and flow of the struggle for Black liberation, self-determination, human rights and a just world. He is more than poet because he chose to be.

Michael Pfleger is a Catholic priest who became a civil rights preacher. He was called to follow the most basic tenets of his faith, to serve and minister to the least of these, those who are hungry, sick, imprisoned, shunned, the oppressed. He heard and heeded that call as he came of age during the Civil Rights Movement, that great mass crusade of Black people and their allies to defeat and dismantle Jim Crow in the south and racist discrimination in the north. He was inspired by that movement and the Christian practice of activists like Dr. King, who were not in pursuit of prosperity for themselves, but freedom for their people. He had been witness to the spiritual force of ordinary people inspired to challenge and confront a seemingly all-powerful enemy. He had heard the songs of freedom, seen domestic workers and laborers, teachers and students, artists and preachers on the march in the spirit of the movement song, *"Ain't Gonna Let Nobody Turn Us 'Round"*. He understood that his faith meant serving the people by fighting for justice and standing with those who need it the most. His ideas, practice and oratorical skills and style were all impacted by what he'd witnessed and was led to dedicate his life to a theology of liberation.

If Father Pfleger had *just* fed the hungry, visited the sick and imprisoned it would have been enough for us, but he chose to be more than a pastor and more than just an ally. He chose to stand with Black people every day, to live and work in his native Chicago's south-side Black community and accept the incredible responsibility of servant leadership as a profound act of his faith.

There was never any doubt that Cornel West's great intellectual capacity, curiosity and discipline could lead him to a life of teaching and writing about any subject he decided to focus on. He devoted himself to Black people, humanity and justice, to study yes, but more importantly to stand with and for. West willed himself in to the position of provocative voice in the discourse on race and justice, theology and the church, politics and morality in America. His writing became required reading on college syllabi, he was a frequent speaker on stages, in pulpits and the media. He is controversial and relentless in his insistence that the liberation needs of Black people were heard by those in power from those who need power. As Black radical intellectuals have historically done, Cornel West has also searched for the form, the organizational tool that could build the political response to assert the demands of a movement for Black liberation and an inclusive democratic society. It is clear that his intention is always to be in the fight. Black people love him even when they disagree with him because they know that like W.E.B. DuBois and Ida B. Wells, Amiri Baraka and Angela Davis, Malcolm, Ella, Martin and so many of our great intellectuals, he is unwavering in his commitment to the transformation of this country and the world into a humane and just place for all the people.

If Cornel had *just* decided to be a teacher and a writer it would have been enough for us. He chose instead to go further, to make himself available to the current of the Black liberation struggle and to flow in it and constantly discover how best to contribute his gifts. In that current he hears the collective voice of history, the profound call of spiritual need and songs of a future promised by our ancestors who chose to live so their children would be born free.

Guided by the poet/scholar Lasana Kazembe, we are invited into this quiet, passionate, and intense conversation between three men whose ideas and work have rescued the lives of some and changed the lives of others. In their reflections and responses you will hear the strength of Harriet Tubman the great conductor of the Underground Railroad who even when weary refused to rest. On these pages are moments of appreciation that they discovered the work that gave their lives purpose. Within their sharp analysis, grounded in decades of experience and study, you may detect subtle frustration that comes from high expectation for themselves and their people. And if we listen closely, it will be evident that this poet, preacher and philosopher are individually and collectively guided by the deep spiritual belief that the march for justice, for the liberation of Black people and humanity is an unstoppable force.

Dr. Michael Simanga

Introduction

What are the Drums Saying?

At the time of this writing, President Donald J. Trump has just waged war with the National Football League, insulted the President and people of Puerto Rico, threatened (via tweet) the people of North Korea with nuclear annihilation, and pushed the envelope even further on the political manipulation and grand scale duping of the American people. Trump's reaction to righteous dissension and legitimate protest is totally consistent with his pattern and practice of intolerance, brutishness, and wholesale endorsement and support of white supremacy and Euro-American nativism. Scholar Henry A. Giroux takes this up in his book, *America at War with Itself.* Trump has used his position to wipe away the specks from the American mirror to render to its citizens (and the world) a more authentic reflection of itself. Naturally, this has caused upset, confusion, denial, and (to the historically informed) affirmation. And then there are the dangerous political overtures by operatives, agents, and cabinet-level folks within the Trump administration that continue to go either unreported or underreported. There is no more room for surprise.

In times such as these, we have always turned to the Ancestors and to venerated, seasoned elders in order to seek their counsel and guidance.

When I sat down with Dr. Cornel West, Fr. Michael Pfleger, and Dr. Haki Madhubuti, I was already deeply familiar with their work, and with their immense (individual and collective) contributions across the last several decades. As one of the most important philosophical voices of the 21st century, Dr. West has had a profound impact on my approach to thinking, argument, and intellectual critique. Reading his work (specifically *Race Matters*, *Democracy Matters*, *Prophecy Deliverance*, and *Black Prophetic Fire*) allowed me to broaden and deepen my appreciation of the Black Freedom Struggle, and to apply that awareness to my teaching and writing. I read Fr. Pfleger's *Radical Disciple* and had visited his parish on numerous occasions through the years, and witnessed firsthand the fruits of love, struggle, and commitment among the faith community of Saint Sabina. My connection with Dr. Madhubuti stretches back a decade or more, and is grounded in deep awareness, respect, and appreciation for his ginormous contributions to education, letters, Black Arts/Black Arts Movement, and Black institution-building.

Every successive generation of people grapples with (or should in some form or another) the critical, political questions of their time. These are organic and ongoing questions of agency, place, space, time, and ultimately, of how we construct, converse, and correspond to/with our true cultural selves. Two areas of scholarship and praxis that continue to fascinate me are 'Maroonage' and the 'Black Radical Tradition.' Maroonage refers to the physical flight and the cultural insistence demonstrated by Africans who escaped the long arm of enslavement. In the modern sense, Maroonage can be taken to refer "ideological" flight – that is, an escape from intellectual confinement and from the limitations imposed by ignorance, prejudice, and hegemony (what late psychiatrist Dr. Bobby Wright termed *'mentacide'*). However, in running from, one is simultaneously running toward. In this case, one is running to truth, to justice, and to become more fully human.

The Black Radical Tradition, a theoretical concept popularized by late political science professor Cedric J. Robinson, refers to the centuries-long arc of Back thought, action, organizing, prophesizing, and collective Black resistance to enslavement, oppression, discrimination, and imperialism.

Among the serious and the thoughtful, this is not tourism or voyeurism. As a professor of education and Africana Studies, I have reminded students constantly about the critical importance of history and of the power of ideas and ideology to shape reality. Relative to this issue, I have two concerns. The first concern is the (seemingly) increasing cultural rift between generations of young and people. Often, the rift is bracketed by tension, mistrust, and impatience. Looking closely, I observe the same unfortunate trends being played out in the broader society, as it becomes easier for people to "relate" to devices and software, and more difficult relate meaningfully with other human beings.

My second concern is two-fold and involves what many have described as a growing anti-intellectualism linked with a disdain for the past (even the recent past). This displays itself in the rapid retreat away from the serious and substantive and toward the material and meaningless. The complex work of reclaiming and recasting the mind and spirit is, in part, what frames the work of Madhubuti, West, and Pfleger. It is sensitive, cultural work which calls for approaches grounded in reality, self-knowledge, and invested in productively serving current and successive generations – most especially the youth. This task demands a vital reclaiming of intellectual and psychic space for the preservation of one's consciousness and being.

The conversation shared in this book is reflective and instructive; it is insightful and intimate. It afforded a rare chance to probe the depth of thinking of three incredible, and accomplished long-distance runners in the struggle for justice and liberation. I am quite honored and extremely humbled with being allowed to facilitate and share in the experience. My deep and undying thanks goes to Dr. West, Fr. Pfleger, and Dr. Madhubuti for sharing their stories.

Dr. Lasana Kazembe

Conversation Part One

Resisting Spiritual Blackout

We now live in one of the most difficult moments in the history of Black people. Although we have known barbaric slavery and vicious Jim Crow, we have never as a people undergone such spiritual blackout. Our ancestors may have been terrorized and traumatized in an unprecedented manner, they had a spiritual and cultural power that made them survive and thrive. In our present moment, even as some have money and others have little money, we are losing our spiritual and moral power. The greatness of Black people is best found in our highly cultivated capacity to love truth, goodness, beauty and the holy. Our spiritual blackout has led too many of us to fall in love with money, status and title and lose connection with what the Isley Brothers call our "caravan of love" or what John Coltrane called "a love supreme". I am so blessed to be in dialogue with my dear brother Dr. Haki Madhubuti – legendary poet, towering educator and long-distance freedom fighter – and my other dear brother Father Michael Pfleger – grand exemplar of the great legacy of Martin Luther King, Jr. We are deeply committed to a revolutionary love that begins with the most vulnerable and poor among us and spills over to every corner of the globe.

This bleak moment of spiritual blackout is inseparable from the decline and decay of the American empire. The long rule of big money, big military and big lies of white supremacy and male supremacy has now unleashed chickens that come home to roost. No oligarchy, no empire and no lies can last forever. We have reached our time of reckoning. And we shall discover who are the all-seasoned-warriors and who are the sunshine soldiers. In times such as these that test the spirits and souls of each and every one of us, we discover who we really are and what we really stand for. The great examples of Frederick Douglass and Harriett Tubman Marcus Garvey and Ida B. Wells-Barnett, Richard Wright and Gwendolyn Brooks, Malcolm X and Ella Baker, Martin Luther King, Jr. and Fannie Lou Hamer, Curtis Mayfield and Nina Simone must inform and inspire each of us to strive for the highest levels of spiritual excellence – reach for courage, fortitude, compassion, and a willingness to live and die owing to our love for the people. Do we have what it takes? We shall see.

Dr. Cornel West
September 7, 2017

Reflections on Resistance and Resilience

LK

In the closing remarks to his 1843 address to the 'Free People of Color' Conference in Buffalo, NY, the honorable Henry Highland Garnet spoke the following:

> *"Let your motto be resistance! resistance! RESISTANCE! No oppressed people have ever secured their liberty without resistance. What kind of resistance you had better make, you must decide by the circumstances that surround you, and according to the suggestion of expediency. Brethren, adieu! Trust in the living God. Labor for the peace of the human race, and remember that you are FOUR MILLIONS."*

Now that was Garnet in 1843. How do you (each of you) interpret those words today, given our current political climate? That is to say, what work lies before us? How is that work to be engaged?

CW

Well, Henry Highland Garnet... he only had one good leg, you know. And he walked around on a crutch. He was physically challenged. Like Ray Charles. Like Art Tatum. And at the same time, we know he was one of the great giants in our tradition. When I hear that though I don't just hear him. I hear Frederick Douglass. I hear Ida B. Wells-Barnett. I hear Marcus Garvey. I hear Sojourner Truth. They're part of a whole tradition; a cacophony of voices telling us to make sure that our humanity and our dignity is viewed as something that must never, ever be violated. No matter what color people are. And in a Trump moment, it means we have to be even more vigilant. This is not the time for sunshine soldiers. We need all-season warriors. Intellectual warriors. Artistic warriors. Spiritual warriors. Political warriors. Across the board. Garnet was a warrior. He was a love warrior, too.

MP
I think we sometimes forget that resistance is absolutely necessary. You cannot accept. You cannot adjust, or assimilate into the wrong. Umm…, so I think resistance always has to be in the forefront whenever we see something that's wrong. You don't ignore. You don't deny. You don't accept it or assimilate into it. But you've got to resist. But I think the other part of it is that resistance has to be rooted in something deeper than you. If our resistance is not rooted in something bigger than us, ummm… there's, I think, the tendency to either become bitter or quit or be compromised. You need a greater strength than yourself. I think the last thing for me would be choosing the tools of resistance. I think it's easy to respond to the lowest common denominator. When we look at our country after 911… everybody went to church the next day. There was no separation of church and state; everyone was on their knees. And then a week later, there was shock and awe; there was violence. That has been our mode ever since. Of shooting, of killing, of dropping drones, and missiles. And so I think that Dr. King comes in and says we have to choose the tools of nonviolence and of truth. And what Dr. West talks is about is choosing love.

Sometimes we lock love into a weakness, but God is love. And I think the tools with which we resist keep us at a high level.

HM

I would agree. I think that one of the real problems in our community, if not most communities, is the lack of historical consciousness. And that as a result of being apolitical and ahistorical, we continue to reinvent the wheel. And as far as Rev. Garnet and others, they were coming out of an enslavement period. Where essentially, in order to move toward liberation, part of the 'road to freedom' process was how do we, as a people, regain our consciousness, essentially because we have been a part of this seasoning process. The enslavement process was taking us from Africa and sprinkling us around the western world to build the western world for people who had committed genocide on another people. And so the people (Indians) who had a genocide committed against them said *"we're not going to work the land that you've taken from us."* And so they brought the Africans here to essentially work the land. But, in order for the Africans to work they land, they had an attempted genocide committed against them (breaking up of families, splitting children from families, spreading us all over the southern U.S., etc.). So what was happening was the breaking down of memory. And so loss of memory forced us to adopt memories from the new surroundings. Unfortunately, those adopted memories included the adoption of white supremacy.

So how do you control a people? You control them by essentially taking everything of value from them (ex., consciousness, bonding traditions, history) and then you force them to become something else. And that happened to us in this country. White supremacy and white nationalism taught us to hate ourselves. Now what Garnet, Douglass, and other great foreparents were doing is encouraging us to work toward regaining a consciousness in this new world. So part of that was not just physical resistance, but the internal resistance to white supremacy. And the goal was for us to come back as a whole people; as an African people. So Garnet's work and ideas are critical. Dr. West mentioned that Frederick Douglass was critical. And most certainly, as we moved into the 20th century and out of the 19th century… you're talking about Booker T. Washington, and W.E.B. DuBois, Ida B. Wells, and so forth. So we have this grand legacy. But the question for all of us is *"How did we end up here and now?"* Nearly 300 years later. Materially, we're a bit offer off. That cannot be argued. But we're still mentally and psychologically wiped out. That's the larger question. Rev. Pfleger is over there in Englewood fighting each and every day. You cannot say that these brothers are just killing each other for just monetary means, or just territory. There's something greater than that. And what's greater than that is that they hate themselves. They don't see this love connection that these Brothers [West and Pfleger] are always talking about. This love connection that we have to have with each other and with our families and with the institutions that we're a part of.

LK

That leads me into something else. It's related. It's definitely related. In ways both normal and remarkable, each of you have received tremendous recognition and done amazing work in your respective vocations and fields. Ok, that's the personal. Throughout it all, you've committed your lives to struggle. Notice I didn't say sacrifice. You've committed your lives to struggle, and to the fight for justice and liberation. Talk about how you've been able to accomplish that and what sorts of challenges you've encountered along the way. That is to say, how have you been able to cultivate yourself in your particular field, but also maintain this life of struggle as activists and blend those two things together in ways that seem so seamless to the outside observer?

CW

Let me first say that, uh, just to set eyes on both of these brothers adds years to my life. Because you can't conceive of what your calling is without having friends, comrades, and family members who sustain you. Everything you do from your dreams, your language, your birth, and your life you are dependent on others. And it's from that *dependence* that you're able to forge your *independence*. But independence is not isolated from being connected to brothers, sisters, moms, dads, traditions, and so forth. So that for me, it has to do with vocation. Vocation is a calling. And a calling is a response to a particular command (in my case as a Christian, it's a command)... I have wonderful secular sisters and brothers, so it could be a demand... The suffering demands you do something about it. Or, [understanding that] Black people are worthy to be loved, and you're willing to serve. That's what Third World Press [Foundation] is about. Fifty years! The Institute of Positive Education. That's what Betty Shabazz School is about. That's what Brother Haki Madhubuti embodies. That's what St. Sabina is about. On the religious side. That demand, or command from God. You are called to be of service. So that the success of the world, y'know, is just fleeting. It doesn't really mean that much. But you use it as a form of weaponry, in terms of what your calling is. And each time I have people who elevate me, I just remember what Brother Malcolm used to say. He said you'll respect me, but you disrespect the brother and sister on the block? If they disrespect the brother or sister on the block, then they can just save their elevation of me.

Because I view myself as an extension of where I came from. The West family, Shiloh Baptist Church, the chocolate side of Sacramento, Glen Elder. That's who I grew up with. That's who loved me. Before the white mainstream or the white establishment. Before Harvard, Yale, Princeton, University of Paris. They were concerned with Little Ronnie. You see? And I'm still that Little Ronnie from where I come from. I was just able to have my calling be manifest in certain places that a mainstream or an establishment gives a lot of authority to. That's why I draw a distinction between a mainstream and a stream. You see, Harvard for me is not mainstream, Harvard is a stream. Harvard hasn't produced a John Coltrane. Harvard hasn't produced a Nina Simone. It hasn't produced a Haki Madhubuti. It ain't produced no Michael Pfleger. Or no John Browns, or Marcus Garveys, or Malcolm Xs, you see what I mean? And I don't say that to put Harvard down, because it did influence DuBois. DuBois is the greatest scholar of us all. But it wasn't Harvard that made him. But he used Harvard as a form of weaponry as he matriculated in solidarity with oppressed people – beginning with Black people, then, of course, connected to others around the world. And that's what my calling is all about. Even though I fall on my face everyday, I try to bounce back.

MP

I guess for me it would be coming in touch with what you think you're here for. And then you have to be willing to not fall into that trap of all the *"I'm ok, you're ok; how to win friend and influence people."* It also means being willing to stand alone and sometimes being willing to be lonely. To be true to yourself. To me, the two most important times in my day are when I wake up in the morning and when I have prayer. I realize that the new day is a gift. And he [God] has put me in positions and I need to be true to those positions, and true to myself and the calling that's been put on me. At the end of the day, when you wash your face and brush your teeth and look in that mirror asking *"Have I lived this day to my best?"* And then repenting for where you haven't or where you've fallen or you've failed. Umm… one should be accountable to God and to self. And then to the people around you. I think something that Dr. West said has always been real key to me. I think your history… and what Dr. Madhubuti brought out about history and then the present that revolves around you. It was me coming in touch with my history that… well… I think that God places you around people and things that form you and you're not even always conscious of it. So, for me, growing up in a house with a sister who was called retarded… to have watched her laughed at and mocked… and then realize that this angered me, as a little six, seven, or eight-year-old kid. And then going into my first year and second year of high school and spending summers with Native Americans and seeing how they were treated. To have walked in a store and hear someone say to me *"Well you can come in, but they can't because they're Indians."* Then seeing Dr. King in Marquette Park and seeing the hate that he experienced from people I saw who went to church, and who lived in my neighborhood, and were respectable people. And then going to the west side and watching the most… well… the organization that was doing most for service on the west side of Chicago in my neighborhood was the [Black] Panthers. Not churches. Not organizations.

And so, I began connecting those dots, and beginning to see what in me was causing something to awaken me to something that was bigger than me… umm… and coming to that understanding in my life that… your life is not about you. I think we live in this really selfish, self-centered mentality. *"What do I get out of it? How's my life any better? What is it gonna do for me?"* We should recognize that it's not about you. It's never been about you. Umm... it's about this long relay race. While you're carrying the baton, what are you going to do. How is somebody's life gonna be better because you lived and you fell? And so it's accepting struggle and... I will use the word 'sacrifice' only because I think that if you're now willing to pay it, then you're unserious about it. I'll never forget when I was in probably my last year of high school. We were getting on a bus to go integrate and protect children at a school. This guy told us before we got on the bus *"if you're not ready to die, then don't get on the bus."* And... I started looking for another bus.

[LAUGHTER]

I'm being honest, you know. But I got on that bus and questioned the seriousness of my commitment and whether I was willing to pay the cost. And pay the price. And do the sacrifice. And to not be accepted. To be on the fringe. To be talked about. To be disliked. To be whatever. And take the hits. Am I willing to do that? And if I'm not then I needed to get off the bus. 'Cause I'm not serious about it. And y'know I look at heroes past and the prices they pay for standing for what they believe.

And then I think like what Dr. West is saying you need people that you look at today... I need the Hakis. I need the Cornels. I need the Belafontes. I need to see people [like the] Farrakhans and the rest of the people who I think stand for what they believe. Umm... I need that council of elders in my life who give witness to that when you get tired. Because it would be foolish to say we don't get tired, or discouraged, or that some days you don't want to say "to hell with it." But then you look at these people and say to yourself

"They're still fighting! How dare you!" Y'know? The Christ I say I believe in didn't quit. So I think you need those folks that you look up to; that inspire you. And not just inspire you, but witness to you. They're living it every day. So it keeps pushing you, y'-know? Like a car you can get in the snow, but sometimes you need a push. Sometimes you need a push. And so, looking at people and having those people that… there's not a whole lot of people I call friends. Y'know cause that's a high bar for me. But these [West and Madhbuti] are friends because of the lives that they live, and their integrity and their truth, and their willingness to pay the price. So I think a combination of that and a combination of being willing to say to yourself that you'll pay the price… that' what roots me in something that holds me accountable. So I can say and ask myself *"I've got this day. How am I living it? How am I using this breath?"*

HM

Y'know… I could just like to comment on something you [Father Pfleger] said. See, you used the word sacrifice as a young man. And there's a profound difference. I think that Jesus the Christ would have never said sacrifice. You were committed. I think there's a profound difference that once we become mature… that we… as young men and women, we make choices within the parameters of other peoples' decisions. So you got appointed to St. Sabina even when the archdiocese was trying to remove you… and you say *"I'm not going."* Okay. And your congregation stepped up and said *"He's not going."* And as you know when you look among the 65 million Catholics, and the way they move the priests around… you've been there over twenty some odd years. So that's a commitment to that church, it's not sacrifice.

MP

Right, right. Right.

HM

As a young man, you can use that term [sacrifice]. But as elders, we make commitments. That was number one. Number two... I think that what has happened in our communities is that we don't know our names. If you don't know who you are, then anybody can name you. And that has happened all throughout our history in this country. And that any people who are in control of their own cultural, political, religious, economic, and social imperatives are about the healthy replication of themselves. That's why we build these institutional structures. Yes, one has family and we can do what we need to do with our families. But when you start talking about fighting, or resistance at a serious level, then you gotta be talking about buiding institutions. Alright? Now I can deal with you [being] at Harvard. Primarily I can deal with you being at Harvard because you do a whole lot of pro bono work. But, many of your brothers and sisters at Harvard are not doing pro bono work. But West is. I know that for a fact, alright? And so, what you have all too often... is that you have ignorant people talking about ignorant other people are. And their ignorant words become the terms of how we develop. So, one can look at a T.D. Jakes and then someone say that's where we need to go. Well, we don't need to go there. We don't need prosperity ministry. We don't need, as men and women, a Creflo Dollar talking about he needs a new jet. Alright? I called the guy and told him I'd send him ten dollars toward [purchasing] the jet if you would get on it and leave and don't come back.

[LAUGHTER]

My point always is that we had mentors who spent time with us. I'm talking about El Hajj Malik el Shabazz (Malcolm X), Margaret and Charlie Burroughs, Dudley Randall (founder of Broadside Press, Detroit, MI), Hoyt W. Fuller (first managing editor of *Negro Digest/Black World* magazine), umm… Barbara Ann Sizemore, one of the premiere educators in this country. In fact, when I was teaching at Howard, Dr. Sizemore became the first Black superintendent of the Washington D.C. public school district. [Her tenure] didn't last long, but they found out that she loved her people too much. And then (in terms of mentors), Gwendolyn Brooks. So what I'm saying is that these mentors in my life saw something in me that I didn't see in myself. But, because they stayed on me… I finally learned that… ok… I got it now. Now it's on me. I gotta keep their names alive. So, all I'm saying at one point is that wherever we land, we gotta make a statement about that which is just, good, right, and correct. All the time. But the best embodiment of those statements are our own lives. And that's critical.

LK

I have a blend of general questions and I have some specific questions for each of you. I'd like to ask a specific question now. But feel free to chime in where you feel inspired. Baba Haki Madhubuti. Your accomplishments in the worlds of art and activism is unparalleled. For decades, you've been an advocate, practitioner, and defender of a strong Black Arts and Black literary tradition. I've heard you say that often. Just what is that? And why is that so vital. Moreover, what is the connection of a strong Black Arts tradition to education and freedom?

HM

Well… I'm here because of art. I was raised in a home where there was none. My mother was one of the most beautiful women in the world. She ended up in the sex trade. Because my father was never there. He was a hustler. He was a gambler. She had to take care of us even though she didn't have a high school education. So she ended up selling her body to take care of me and my sister. At 14, she asked me to go to the Detroit Public Library to check out *Black Boy* by Richard Wright. And I had refused to go because I hated myself. And this hatred was based upon primarily my color, and how poor we were, and the lack of stability in our lives. But I went and got the book. I didn't ask the white librarian because I hated myself and I didn't feel right going to a white library to ask for a book written by a Black man who was critical of white America. So, I found the book on the shelf, and then I went to an unpeopled section of the library and sat down and began to read. I was 14. It was the first time in my life that I was reading a book that was not anti-Black. I was reading a book that was essentially pro-me. So, I read half the book at the library, then took it home and finished it that night. I finished it in less than twenty-four hours, and then gave it to my mother the next day. Then I went back to the library and checked out everything that Richard Wright had published. Now, this was the first time I was introduced to ideas. Serious ideas. And those ideas kept me awake. They just kept me awake. I was reading everything Richard Wright had published. He had published a book entitled *White Man, Listen*. That book is a book of essays dealing with psychology, Black literature, and so forth. And in his essay on Black literature, he had mentioned all these Black writers.

So that was my template to begin to really read into us. So, at 14 and 15, I'm systematically reading Claude McKay, Du Bois, William Monroe Trotter, y'know? I'm systematically going through all of these great minds. And, as a result of that, I'm now a different person. Because back then, music had been the most profound thing for me. Music was just saving my life. Not only doo-wop, but also jazz. I mean Louis Armstrong was the baddest thing out there. He could play trumpet, compose, and so forth. And for me, Louis Armstrong was the greatest musician, but I didn't care for his mannerisms. Even though, Armstrong, unbeknownst to most people, was a radical as you get. Ok? Another thing is that… a man by the name of Miles Davis came on the scene. And Miles Davis was black, clean… I mean, women gravitated toward Miles Davis and his playing like he was a free shoe store.

[LAUGHTER]

And so, all of this starts with art. Art was critical in terms of my young life. My mama was brought into the sex trade by a black minister. And that destroyed me a great deal. He had one of the biggest churches in Detroit. Rev. Wright. That was his name. And we lived in the basement apartment of one of his apartment buildings. [My mother] was the janitor. She'd take garbage cans down and have my 11-year old sister help her out, and all that stuff. But this guy would visit her twice a week. He told her never to come back to his church. So we left Little Rock [Arkansas] and came to Inkster, Michigan. We stopped there and my dad had lost all our money. So, he left us, and we went up to Detroit. When we arrived there, people would always ask us if we had a home church. We never had a home church, so we ended up at Rev. Wright's church. [My mother] used to sit in the front pew, and this guy couldn't take his eyes off of her. I mean it was just embarrassing. And as walked out, he was whispering in her ear. And the next thing you know we were moving into his apartment building. So, that didn't last that long, obviously. He [Rev. Wright] went to the National Baptist Convention, and was on the podium. He somehow fell off and was killed. Joseph Jackson was there. They were running for the presidency [of the National Baptist Convention]. So when he died, his wife put us out, and then my mother got into having to sell herself. She had at first been selling herself to the minster, but then she started selling herself to the general population. But she had told me to go and get *Black Boy* and I was already into music... that's where I said I'd like to spend my life and try to do something. It's a really long story. But, art was critical for me in terms of... um... well.. one thing about religion, since I have these two religious brother here...

[LAUGHTER]

I believe... I believe in all religions. See, when I travel – and this is why travel is so important – when I travel, I travel to the spiritual houses of wherever I'm going. Ok? So I've been to Africa eighteen times. I've been to Europe. I've been to Asia. I've been to South and Central America. I've been to every state in the United States expect for Hawaii, Alaska, and the Dakotas. So I'm a listener, and I'm a visitor. And I say that most of these religions are right, and they're wrong. They're right in the good that they teach, and the message that they bring that allows people to elevate themselves, free their minds, and become liberated individuals within the context of the spiritual force. But they're wrong when they say that "this is the only way... and there's no other way." That's how you wind up with a Jim Jones. And so, for me, that's why I can deal with these brothers [Pfleger and West] because I have no problem in understanding the goodness in them, and what they're doing. Because I'm trying to do the same thing on a spiritual side and even on a secular side, but I will never, at any level, argue or speak against what they are doing within the context of their spiritual force. Because it's critical for their lives, and it's critical for my life, too, in order for me to be connected to them. 'Cause we gotta believe in something.

LK

And so, the artists you mentioned; the musicians… you're linking them and their tradition to freedom in what ways?

HM

Well… John Coltrane was very spiritual. Ok? And, as quiet as its kept, so was Langston Hughes. And Paul Robeson. I mean, the people who proceeded us… they had a spiritual core. They may not have articulated it in the way that I articulate it, because we're generations away from them. And I think that for me, travel has just been so important. Because I've seen the spiritual path that people take work all over the world. This is why I will never entertain atheism or agnosticism. For me, it always comes back to this question: *"Where is your core?"* So I'll meditate and do yoga. They [Pfleger and West] may say prayer, but it's really the same thing at one level. I'm trying to look at a world picture. For instance, I'm trying to understand how the great majority of the world's population are suffering. The great majority of the world's population of children are going to bed hungry every night. Alright? So therefore, how do we, in our own minor way, bring some help, some relief to any of this. And so, I try in my own minor way. That's why I think that what we're trying to do with this book is to show that there can be these connections – and they're love connections – but, they're connections that we go into with our eyes wide open… recognizing that we might not agree one hundred percent. But I tend to think we're in the ninetieth percentile.

LK

Ok, ok. Well... Dr. Cornel West... you're all too aware of the precarious and the dangerous state of affairs that we're facing these days, especially on the national scene. In your book, *Prophecy and Deliverance*, you describe Afro-American history as the story of a "gallantly persistent struggle." You go on to describe that our "cultural response to injustice, white paternalism, post-industrial capitalism, etc. has meant the maintenance of self-respect in the face of pervasive denigration." In light of today's challenges, what specific ways do you see Black people responding now? I mean, I just quoted a statement you wrote in your book, which was written before the era we're in now. So I'm wondering what your present takeaways might be.

CW

Yeah, Brother. I appreciate the question. That book was written thirty-five years ago. And we were in deep crisis then, and it's worse now. I fundamentally believe that the Black freedom movement is the greatest tradition in the modern world. There's been no people who have been so hated for 400 years. Incessantly hated. And yet, we've taught the world so much about how to love. There's been no people who've been so terrorized, traumatized, and stigmatized daily. For 400 years. In the middle of a nation that understands itself as a beacon of liberty. And we must have fortitude. Now fortitude is not the same as courage. A Nazi soldier can be courageous in the face of fear. But courage has a spiritual and a moral dimension. Fortitude is the fusion of courage with magnanimity; with greatness of character. Brother Haki talks about Louis Armstrong... that's fortitude. He's a genius. He's got courage. But he's building on the tradition going all the way back through spirituals on the slave plantations. He's using a European instrument, but he's playing African rhythms in the New World context with a European instrument. Coltrane's doing the same thing with a sax. Created by Adolph Sax in Belgium, 1948.

So you say what is it about these people, and this tradition? Well you see, Aunt Esther dies in the eighties in the ten-play cycle of August Wilson. She was born 1619. She dies in 1985. I asked Brother August, *"Are you telling me that the great tradition of spiritual integrity and collective resistance and moral authority that we Black people have brought, not just to America, but to the world, is dying?"* See, that brings tears not just to our eyes – all three of us – but to the eyes of Ida. And Marcus. And Martin. And Malcolm. And Fannie. And Ella Baker. Ella Fitzgerald and Ella Baker. Why? Because when you have a Sankofa sensibility, then you know you can't really move forward unless you connect with the best of the past. So that lack of historical consciousness that Brother Haki is talking about, in the present moment... not enough connection to the best – not just of who we are – but the best in the modern world. See Martin King... see he's a human being; he's flawed, but it's hard to find analogues of Martin King in other cultures. There's a whole lot of oppressed people who've been hated. Martin King's a love warrior in the way that Coltrane was. He's a love warrior the way Sarah Vaughn was. The smile that she had. The connection that she had with everybody. Coming from the chocolate side of Newark, New Jersey. Mt. Zion Baptist Church. That's what's being lost. And that's one reason why America is becoming neo-fascist.

See, without the Black Freedom Struggle, America would have gone neo-fascist a long time ago. We are the leaven in the American loaf. We're the leaven in the democratic tradition. If it wasn't for the Black Freedom Struggle, America would have neo-fascist across the board. Not just to indigenous people. Not just to us. Our movement gets weak, our music gets weak, our families get weak, our communities get weak, our churches get weak… all of them become commodified. Then you lost your leaven in your loaf. And you end up with Trump. Gangsta. To. The. Core! Grabbing women's private parts? That's gangsta. 'Gon take somebody else's oil? Iraq? That's gangsta! That's what it is to use your arbitrary power in order to procure your own little selfish ends. Black people have been dealing with gangsta America for 400 years. But without our leaven – and that's getting weaker – the whole nation now has a spiritual blackout.

And so our task – especially as older brothers… and that's what we are… we're old school brothers… which is to say, we are preserving the best of the best tradition in the modern world. But, it's hard to pass it on to the younger generation because they have been so commodified, commercialized, marketized, and brainwashed to think that life is just about the next pleasure. About the next commodity. It's about status. It's about celebrity. See, all of that is spiritual blackout. That's spiritual blackout. If Curtis Mayfield had been banking on winning a Grammy, we would have missed one of the greatest geniuses in the last thirty-five years. So he never wins a Grammy, but Milli Vanilli wins two. We don't give a damn about Milli Vanilli. Look at Curtis. He drops out as a high school sophomore and goes on to produce some of the greatest art of the twentieth century. He's from the west side of Chicago. And Curtis is alongside a host of others. But I think that he's one of the, the, the towering ones. But he knows that he's part of this grander tradition. So, when we talk about the present moment, it's back to Henry Highland Garnet. How do you resist and have fortitude? Courage and greatness of character. And not just the great name, either.

We're talking about everyday people who have this. Folk on the ground. Folk in the barbershops and beauty salons. Ain't no Curtis without his grandmother. You see? There's no Haki Madhubuti. Not just for the towering figures like Gwendolyn Brooks. But the folks who love him before he me Gwendolyn. Whose names the world might not ever know. Same is true with Brother Pfleger. I knew his father. He used to sit in that wheelchair right on that front row. Every Sunday. Loving this brother to death. And they were the only two vanilla brothers in the whole church.

MP

But my father always made sure that I understood. When he came to see you speak at St. Sabina, my father would say to me *"don't make me choose between you, my son, and Cornel West. Because I prefer Cornel West."*

l to r: Fr. Michael Pfleger, William Allen, Lasana Kazembe, Cornel West, Haki R. Madhubuti

Conversation Part Two

Healing Spiritual Laringytis

As I look at the state of America, Illinois, and Chicago, and the dysfunction and the brokenness of which our city, state and country are now in, it seems urgent to me that the faith community gets healed from its spiritual laryngitis and regain our prophetic voice. We have lost our moral compass and seemingly in America our conscious. And while the faith community has become silent, there are those under the banner of faith who have sought to become the theologians for Pharaoh and give affirmation and approval to evil and a second breath to the worst of America.

One thing we must thank Donald Trump for is that he has pulled back the rug on the real America that we pretend does not exist. We must be sure not to be bamboozled by the distractions of conversations about statues and cartoons and ignore the roots of racism that have given our children failed schools and our neighborhoods economic deserts and made no changes in African Americans getting contracts, sitting on boards, being the most still incarcerated and most unemployed, allowing our communities to look like third world countries.

While hate, division, and lies rise up boldly, so must truth, love and unity become just as bold, and just as strong. We must as faith communities refuse to join our wagons to either Democrats or Republicans, rather become independent and married to the party of truth freedom and justice. As Dr. Martin Luther King, Jr. told us, "there are times when silence become betrayal" and so are the times in which we now live.

The faith communities must once again take the side of the poor and the disenfranchised and allow them to not only find a friend in us but a fearless lobbyist and advocate as well. We must demand and give mercy to care for those neglected, but we must also demand justice so as to dismantle the systems that have created the poverty and the abandonment.

It is time for the faith communities to come together and put aside egos and differences and join in the common bond of truth and our care for the poor.

Fr. Michael Pfleger
September 5, 2017

Reflections on Art, Culture, and Struggle

LK

Ok, Father Michael Pfleger. Now, it's been written that your "A-ha!" or awareness moment came about in the wake of the riots and the looting after Dr. King was assassinated. In your book *Radical Disciple*, it's mentioned that you were among a crowd of people who had been on the block the morning after the looting happened. People were looking around at the firebombed cars, the burned-out buildings, and the bricks and the rubble. And an old woman was out there with all of you and she said *"Time to clean up. Time to start going forward."* In the book, you describe that you took her words as a message that was meant for you. My question to you is are you still hearing that message? And, if so, in what ways are you hearing it?

MP

Umm. Yeah. That's what struck me when I went out that next morning. Watching this elderly woman. Elders have a wisdom. And a plain truth that doesn't get caught up with all the rest. They just speak right from their spirits, and their hearts. So, she was out there in the street with a broom. And there's rubble everywhere but she had this one little broom. And, as she started sweeping the street she said *"Time to clean up. What are we gon' do now?"* And what struck me about that and what was so powerful is that… um… I was devastated over the assassination of Dr. King. Because I really looked forward to joining his movement and going to work with King full time. That's what I wanted to do. But then, everything that had inspired me since I was a junior in high school… had just been wiped out. And the big question was *"so what are you going to do now?"*

We should also understand that we should never get held hostage by our anger, or our frustrations, or by our circumstances and situations. We should always realize that the possibilities are always greater than the problem. And that tomorrow always represents an opportunity that the past can't rob from you. So, what are we going to do now? What are we going to try to do to make a difference? And it's funny… we were talking about the young brothers and sisters… I'll go and I'll stand or march with brothers and sisters on the street, or in front of the police station, or down to Michigan Avenue. But then the question returns: *"What are we going to do now?"* After we've expressed our anger and outrage, which is important and real. But, what are we going to do constructively to make a change so that we don't keep coming out to the same form of reference? There's more to it than that. So, we have to now take the moment and figure out how we're going to transform this. And that was always important to me. I remember when I first became pastor at St. Sabina. The first thing we did was call a meeting of the community. We asked the community "What do you need us to do, because we're here to serve you. We're not here to be an oasis in this community, or to exist separately from this community. We're here to serve this community. So we had several meetings where we asked the people to tell us the things we need to hear. Because I always remember that I'm white. I'm always a guest in somebody else's community. I never forget that. You can't ever know somebody's community or experience better than they do. I'm always ready to learn. And so everything we built out of our community… from the social services center to the senior center… whatever we've done has come about as a result of the community saying *"we need this and we want this."* And so, that woman's voice continues to haunt me consistently because every time I get overwhelmed with a situation…. no matter… without fail… I mean… I remember right after this last [presidential] election… there were so many people who called me right after the election and they were wondering what happened. And they sounded as though they were losing their faith; that they were shaken and fearful, discouraged, overwhelmed… and that's a real moment that we have to embrace and not try to deny. But then, ok, how do we handle this moment? And what do we do because of this moment. How do we avoid just surrendering to the moment? That right there has always been one of my constant struggles in life. We can never assimilate; we can never adjust to darkness. But that's so easy to do. We sometimes get up at night; we don't want to really wake up, so we feel our way in the dark and our eyes begin to adjust to the dark. Recently, someone asked me *"what's the one important thing that you tell to seminary students?"* And I said *"turn on the light. Turn on the light and stop adjusting to darkness. Stop praying about the darkness. Stop waiting for the by-and-by. Turn on the light today, face the issue and the problem, and deal with it."*

We've got create what's ahead of us, and not let what's ahead of us dictate to us.

HM
Why'd you become a priest?

MP

Well, I went to the local high school which was a seminary leadership school, and it was the nicest school around, offered a good education, and was walking distance from my house. So let's be real clear. It was Quigley South at 77th Western. When I read the experiences... and when I sat down with Native Americans, I saw their rich spiritual depth, and it took me to another level. But then, I saw Dr. King during my junior year of high school (1966). I see him... and I see all this hate and all this anger... and I see him not responding to any of it. I didn't even know at that point that he'd already been hit with a rock [in Marquette Park, Chicago]. So, I'm watching him and I'm riding my bike home with two friends, and I'm so conscious of that day that I remember like it was yesterday and I remember myself thinking there's something about this man that either he's crazy or he has some kind of power I don't know about. So, I started to read everything about him. I was cutting out newspaper articles and pasting them on the walls of my room. And, one of things that struck me so much about him was when he said that we [the U.S.] could pass laws to make lynching illegal, but we can't pass laws that transform the heart. King insisted that that's something that has to come from our faith and from something bigger than us; our spirituality; our spirit. And so, I wanted to change hearts, not simply laws. I think we have to fight laws to change laws, but to me that was still a band-aid until we change people. And, when people say to me "Why are you a priest because of a Baptist minister?" But King taught me the power of faith. And I think what was so striking to me was that my experiences with religion up to that point were kind of a joke, or a game, or just this ritual. Y'know, just this religious thing that you went through without getting in touch with its power. So, Dr. King taught me the power of faith. And, I wanted to tap in... I wanted to create a church where… y'know I always said when I was going through seminary school that if I ever became a pastor, that I would create a church that modeled the blueprint he left. One that modeled the power of faith and not the escape from life.

HM

I think that's what's missing all too often our biographies. I mean for all of us. For you [speaking to West], why'd you choose education? And how did you end up matriculating through the top universities? And what have been your battles at those universities? It seems to me that there's a personal price that you pay with all of this.

CW

I've always looked at the musicians as the vanguard of the species. So, I couldn't sing like Luther Vandross. I couldn't play drums like the late, great Clyde Subblefield. I couldn't move as fast as James Brown. I can move, but not that fast. I wanted to do what the musicians did in the life of the mind. When I was growing up, that's what the model was. It was The Delfonics, it was The Dramatics, it was The Chi-Lites, it was The Whispers and The Main Ingredient. Those were the ones that for me exemplified levels of excellence. And so, growing up in Shiloh [Baptist Church], I'd hear nothing but music. And we had a great pastor. And the Black Panther Party was right next door [in Oakland, CA]. So I'm connected to their breakfast programs and connected to what they're doing and what they're reflecting. All of that was filtered through my Christian formation. And so, when I decided to go to Harvard, it was clear to me that the reason why I had access to Harvard is because the Black masses had rebelled in responding to the death of Brother Martin. And now the white elite structures had opened up possibility, and their aim was to co-opt and incorporate a Black middle class that would hide and conceal the suffering of the masses. But that Black middle class would not have expanded without those rebellions taking place. And those rebellions were different even than the demonstrations. That Black rage during the rebellion was different than the calm demonstrations. You get Black poor folk reaching their absolute limit and boiling over. That's the after effect of Brother Martin's death.

So, when I got to Harvard, I went straight to work for the [Black Panther's free] breakfast program, and then to Norfolk prison where I taught for three years. I became co-president of the Black Student Association, and from them on that's what my vocation has always been. I think one of the things that always upset me though (and this is where I've encountered a lot of problems) is that I knew that the white power structure would have a certain kind of attitude toward folk who sided with Black folk, poor people, and so forth. But, I saw Black folks who seemed to be bitten by the bugs of conformity, and complacency, and cowardice. And so, when we would refer to this as the American empire, rather than just a democracy, there'd we'd get in trouble. You see it nowadays on the Palestinian question. It's a sad thing to see, Black cowards not being explicit about [the plight of the Palestinian people]. You got 500 [Palestinian] babies killed within fifty days and not one major Black spokesperson can say a mumbling word because they're scared. See, that's cowardly. That's not what we were taught. We ought to be morally consistent. A Palestinian baby has the same value as a Jewish baby, a Black baby, a Brown baby, and so forth. And so, I encountered that [Black cowardice] very early. It was clear that there were very narrow constraints where certain kind of things could be safe. If you went outside of those constraints… BAM! You're out! Now the beautiful thing was that my savior went outside of those constraints. Jesus, I mean. He was a phonetical prisoner. He was a criminal who was killed by the Roman Empire. He ran the money-changers out of the temple. These days, that temple is a combination of White House, Pentagon, state house, Hollywood, and Wall Street. Who's running those folk out of the temple? See what I mean? And so, that [Jesus] legacy, is one that I was able to have access to very, very early. And I received so much love. You [Haki] and I have fascinating juxtapositions. I had so much love coming at me from age zero to seven, but I was still a gangsta. And you were able to make and remake yourself in such a magnificent way with… not a whole lot of love gas in your tank. You had some, but not a whole lot. And you encountered these giants [Dudley Randall, Gwendolyn Brooks, etc.] later. But I had so much love coming at me from zero to seven, and it continues on up to this very day. So, in that sense, it's fascinating how we end up on the exact same love train with very different kind of tributaries leading to that train. For me, it was really a life of the mind. books and this black musical sensibility that we use a kind of form of weaponry.

HM
You know, all of our lives touch because of a single person. I was in all of the marches with King. I was in Marquette Park.

CW & MP
You were there? Really?

HM
Yeah. I was there. In fact, the person I was holding hands with was a white man. Really. In Marquette Park. I was a foot soldier. It was

1966 and I had just published *Think Black*. So, the Catholic Church had been a very important part of my own maturation. Because of what my mother was going through with her... well... she had become a drug user and an alcoholic. And she had sold her body for the last time because the guy killed her. He beat her up so badly we couldn't have an open casket. But, prior to that, there was a church [in Detroit] called St. Stanislaus that I would go to. I write about it in *Yellow Black*. The churches were big, and quiet, and clean all the time. But, be that as it may, I left the church for any number of reason. But the thing that's really important is that King was such an important connection to all of us. I was a Malcolm man, but at the same time, you could not deny the bravery, the insight, the total commitment of King. Even when he got the Nobel Prize, he didn't take the money for himself. That's what has always affected me a great deal. So, for me, as we talk and think about this whole history of struggle and resistance, we have to understand that nothing will happen, unless we resist. And you two brothers represent for me the epitome of national and international struggle. Having that spirit of resistance is so critical now, because we're in the 21st century, we have a Neanderthal, pedophile, misogynist in the White House. And he's surrounded by real criminals who no longer have to put a sheet over their heads. So, white supremacy and white nationalism have become the public forum for them to push their ideas.

LK

That's so important. As we move on, I would like to understand from each of you what is your vision of tomorrow. What do you see and what do we need to do?

CW

I think we've moved from a neoliberal era with Obama. And don't forget the 26,000 bombs he dropped in just one year during 2016. And in the U.S.'s budget, fifty-four cents of every dollar go to military spending. So, it's an empire.

HM

So, it's not a defense budget, it's an offense budget?

CW

That's exactly right. This military industrial complex is always on the offense because we have a permanent war economy. Perpetual preparation for war to keep the arms industry in play, and to subjugate other people. But as bad as that [neoliberal era] was, this neofascist era is worse because we're seeing an escalation of the military budget, the bombs, and the drone strikes. And on top of that, we see the transfer of wealth from poor and working-class people to the top one-percent. Under Obama, the top one-percent received over eight percent of the income growth. But nobody really talks about that. Under Trump, it'll likely be ninety-five percent. So, it'll get worse, but it's already bad. And don't get me wrong, it was in place under Reagan and Clinton. It's just with Obama we thought we were going to get some King-like legacy, as opposed to the same old thing. So symbolically, we were breakdancing on the ground and sleepwalking. And what this means is, now our habits of resisting the status quo are weaker. So many people these days are defending the status quo. The flag-waving people. The cross-bearing people.

But, we have the Movement for Black Lives. That's a sign of hope. A crucial sign of hope. I think the younger generation is hungry for resist, resist, resist in a way that puts a smile on my face. What I really see is the domino tendency of these male fascists in the United States. They seem to have tendencies that are just as ugly as fascists we tend to see over the in the Middle East and Africa. Then we have AFRICOM expanding throughout various parts of Africa. The right-wing movement in Latin America. In that sense, the call for resistance that [Henry Highland] Garnet called for becomes even more pressing. Even more pressing.

MP
Well, just to return to the point about resistance, we cannot allow a Trump or a Trump agenda to control the narrative. But, I think that's what is happening right now. We are seeing this country reacting to the agenda he's setting. And, we've got to stop reacting to that. I think we've got to set the agenda and not react to his agenda. We also should see this as a moment of opportunity, both for opposition and to connect.

One of the dangerous things I'm afraid of right now is that he's become so aggressively evil that people are starting to fight for survival in their silos. So Muslim brother and sisters are fighting in their silo; Latino brothers and sisters are fighting in their silos; brothers in the community fighting here, Black Lives Matter folks here, etc. So, everybody's into this survival mode, which gives power to the oppressor. And we're not survivors, we're conquerors. So we need to connect the pain. Y'know, for me the truth of the matter is that… one of the ways Trump got elected is because Democrats and Republicans have failed and people are anti-government. He got elected on white nationalism; white male nationalism, in particular. Trump started this thing over eight years ago with that birtherism movement. It was really not about

Obama's birth certificate at all, but about the fact that they felt Obama was not one of them. So they gave it a racial undertone and kept it going for eight years. So, Trump tapped into the anger, and white nationalism, and racism. He tapped into all of that and connected to the angry miner, and the angry Appalachian, and angry folks throughout this country. And personally, I listened to folks from the African American community who said stuff like *"I like his candor and his honesty."* But were they listening to what he was actually saying? So we need to tap into that anger with power and the opportunity to direct because we're always responding to it. Government was not ever set up to serve the masses. It was set up to protect itself. And so, one thing that's going on now is the exposing of the evilness of the power structure. So, in this moment comes the opportunity for us to say we have stop relying on the power structure, and stop letting it direct us. We have to say *'No'* and decide that we're going to direct it, and set the agenda, and make the power structure respond to us. So I think there is an opportunity amidst all the ugliness of it, but I think we have to connect these silos. We must not let this Trump administration divide us, and conquer us. Evil, hatred, racism, prejudice, sexism... we're all connected to that. And so this is the time to come together let our pain unite us and not separate us.

CW

Indeed. Solidarity is crucial. The multiracial coalition against fascism. One quick thing I would add and that is the ugly role of the corporate media. For a year-and-a-half, they covered every speech he [Trump] gave. Every tweet. Every comma. Every period. Every sentence. And they did it for money purposes. Remember what the head of CBS [Leslie Moonves] said: Trump *"may be bad for the country, but it's damn good for CBS."* The profits went up fifty percent across the board. It's not just FOX News. We know how reactionary they are. CNN, MSNBC, all of them did that. So that for every eighty-six minutes that Trump got, Bernie Sanders got twenty-something seconds. If Bernie had been exposed in that way, at least we could have had a broader discussion about poverty, Wall Street, and so forth.

So in going back to resistance, you got Third World Press Foundation, and the Institute for Positive Education trying to keep alive certain stories. But they're dealing with an avalanche of the lies coming through corporate media. So we have to really make sure the children will be equipped to keep track of the lies coming their way. The lies hide crimes. Mendacity is tied to criminality, you see? And with institution-building, Brother Haki has been engaged in that work for fifty years. Overall though, we have weak institutional capacity. How do we get our stories out, especially when the corporate media is so predominant with its stories that are mendacious? So the reason why Trump can't stand the press is because, as a gangster, he knows they have the same ends as he does and that they're trying to get over. And so they gave him every minute and he knows they only did it for profits. So he really has no respect for the media now. He manipulated them and played them the way Paganini played the violin. It's true. And part of our challenge is to understand that resistance is necessary, but not sufficient. We've gotta resist, but how do we forge institutional capacity to tell our stories – especially to young people – in the face of corporate media?

HM

In 1973, I wrote a book called *From Plan to Planet*. I was trying to deal with the developing world. For me, it's not what you're against, but what you're for. And this is one of the reasons we really got into this institution-building. Essentially, we can resist without thinking. Resistance [in and of itself] is an honorable response. But, it still leaves the question, *"What do we do now?"* What is missing within the context of our community are independent Black institutions that work at every level of human involvement: finance, education, entertainment, etc. There are 86,000 Negro churches – and I use the term 'Negro' advisedly. Out of 86,000 Negro churches, there might be 1,000 Black churches. There are over one million Black and Brown men locked down in these prisons. The average Black or Brown brother in these prisons cannot even read at a sixth grade-level. If you can't read at a sixth grade-level, then you can't write at a third or fourth grade-level. What are they going to do once they get out of prison? There's nothing for them to do in a scientific, technological, knowledge-based world. Nothing. So they enter an underground economy that was created by the corporate class, you see?

Black people in Chicago are relegated to roughly 75-80 blocks on the south-and west-sides of this city. There's no industry. None. What are they going to do? So, the interesting thing around this Trump phenomena – and it was in the news recently – *"White Deaths of Despair Surge in U.S."* Even in the Financial Times, they're writing about Appalachia and white poor communities citing how they're no jobs, no more middle class, and how [whites] are hooked on drugs and dying at higher rates than Black and Brown people in the U.S. But, at the same time, you cannot even go into these communities and tell them that Trump is their enemy. Even though the folks from those communities jumped on Hillary [Clinton], though she wasn't my ideal candidate either. She took hundreds of thousands from Goldman-Sachs for speeches, and now Trump has predictably surrounded himself with Gold-Sachs executives.

If you look at the latest issue of *Forbes* (the billionaire issue), they write about it being a record year for the ultimate rich. According to *Forbes*, there are over 2,043 billionaires in the United States with a net worth of $7.7 trillion. If you take the combined wealth of Bill Gates, Warren Buffet, and the Walton family, that's more combined wealth of, most certainly, the Black community, if not most of the U.S. The key point we have to understand is how do we begin to earn wealth in this criminal operation. So we have to become guerilla warriors; to grapple with the challenge of how we go about creating serious money and then using it within the context of our own communities, while also not violating our values. So I don't know anything about Wall Street, but we have brothers and sisters who do. How do we get to them? But to get back to something that was mentioned earlier… and I write about this in *Taking Bullets*… there's this man named Chalmers Johnson who wrote a trilogy entitled *Blowback*. He writes about America's black sites, and it's several hundred military bases around the world. Therefore, it's like we said earlier, your defense budget is an offense budget. All over the world. Most people don't know that. So, we can't come out here and just keep telling people this same nonsense. I know a minister who's name I won't call. But he's very popular and has been around for a long time. Even worked as one of King's key lieutenants. I was on a program with the guy and we were working with some prisoners. So, as we were trying to get it started, the prisoners just kept talking among themselves, and the administrators could not quiet them down. So this minister just said two words and everybody stopped what they were doing and got quiet. He said *"Let's pray."* So they stopped. My point is, is that as diehard as some of these brothers are, there is still this spirit inside them because most of them were raised in the church. They left it after being betrayed by the church. So what we're trying to suggest is that there is another way, but that way has got to encourage people to ask questions about what they're trying to do, what they're trying to build, and what is important to them. I mean because we're up against great odds. It must be understood that communities which are in control of their own cultural imperatives at every level of human involvement are taking care of their babies. We gotta have men and women who are conscious and who are willing to do that. Not only in terms of the primary, elementary, and high, but all the way up through the university. I've seen the kinds of treachery that plays out through all of the systems. So, part of our responsibility is that you gotta show what works. If you don't have anything out there that's working, then you'll always have these charlatans who can come and talk a good game. You can't beat these guys speaking. I've seen it time and time again. So, one of the reasons I love Mike [Pfleger] so much is that he's got St. Sabina, and the housing over there. You have the businesses in the community. The schools. You can't argue against that.

CW

And the same is true with institutions, too.

MP

Yeah, yeah. Something you mentioned that is so important that I still say is that the greatest institution that has failed America is not corporate, or educational. It is the faith community. That's where the conscience ought to be awakened. Whether we're talking about King or Malcolm, we're talking about people who were deeply rooted and used their faith to be the prophetic voice. We now have these pimps in pulpits. Who, indeed, will say *"let's pray"* instead of *"let's act."* Malcolm and King used their faith for action, and for transformation, and for confrontation. And today, whether you're talking about the church, the mosque, or the synagogue, the pulpits have become weak and compromised. They push a cotton candy theology and they are part of the Fortune 500! They're part of the mainstream! We gotta remember the history of the church. The Black preachers used to be the most educated. And now, they're some of the least educated.

HM
But they've been called though?

MP
But they've been called. Who was on that phone we don't know! But they've been called.

[LAUGHTER]

And so now we've seen the pulpit become the tool of the enemy. I get so angry. I say this at every church I go to. When I see a picture of Dr. King [in other churches], I ask them "How are you living like him… beyond hanging a picture up of him in your study or in your church?" King is so fundamental to who I am. So, when I see people bastardizing him it angers me. And the faith community has been bought, and it no longer is a prophetic voice. I believe part of the killing of Martin was to send a message to ministers. I think that's why we didn't see somebody step up who should have. They said *"I don't want to have what happened to King happen to me."* I saw that with Jeremiah Wright. I kept saying in 2008… I spoke to over 200 preachers and I told them *"you are standing down and letting Jeremiah Wright be persecuted. And you don't even understand that this is about you."* They were sending a message with Jeremiah Wright saying *"this is what's gonna happen to your ass if you start saying the things he's saying."* It's the same thing they're doing to Colin Kapernick right now. With the [NFL] owners. They're sending a message. They talk among themselves and decided they were going to blackball him. The same thing they did to Craig Hodges.

HM
Whiteball.

MP
Yeah, yeah. Whiteball.

[LAUGHTER]

I stand corrected. But, they're sending these messages, and the problem is the majority have run with the message. You see athletes being silent. How many of them have you seen come out and support Colin? How many came out in support of Craig Hodges? Or Jeremiah Wright? Black, white, or brown? It didn't happen because they didn't want to become a target. And then, at the same time they were living in fear, you had the corporations and the powerful come in to entice them and bribe them. And now, they've become the very enemy that they were talking about before. They're the enemy now.

CW
Let me just say a quick word about education. My dear brother hit this hard, but I just want to make a distinction between being educated and having a degree. We know Malcolm was highly educated, yet he had no degree. Degrees can play an important role, but there's a fetishizing of degrees that we see among the preachers.

They all got to be doctors. Everybody's a doctor. *"Where'd you get your degree? Well I got it through the mail. Studied for a couple of days, then showed up for the commencement."*

[LAUGHTER]

So they're ascribing magical powers to the degrees, and that's part of a cultural, superficial spectacle where it's the simulation and the simulacrum rather than the real thing. And as long as you have a semblance of it, then you perceive. But when we talk about education, we're really talking about a love of mind and curiosity, a wrestling with complexity, and, most importantly, fortitude – courage and greatness of character. We do have an educated class that is still profoundly niggerized. They have these degrees, and these positions, but they're still scared, intimidated, afraid, and they're subject to manipulation and incorporation because they're for sale. They can come out of the highest institutions of higher learning, but they're not really educated – they're credentialized. Absolutely. And in that sense, we're looking for the deeply educated ones that are coming in the same traditions as the Curtis Mayfields, Malcolm Xs, and Fannie Lou Hamers, as well as the Du Bois, the Paul Robesons, the Haki Madhubutis, and others.

HM
Well the negroes are back in charge.

CW
Indeed so, brother. That's what you said in your eulogy for the great Amiri Baraka. I was sitting right there in the audience. I looked over at the casket and said *"Amiri, the negroes are back in charge."* And I think what that means for many of us relates back

to something Marcus Garvey said: *"As long as Black people are in America, the masses of Black people will live lives of ruin and disaster."* That is the challenge coming out of a Black nationalist tradition. There will be space for Black middle class negroes who decide to become well-adjusted to injustice. Now, Du Bois got on a boat and told his friend *"Cheer up, the Negroes can never win in America."* He knew we had to move on an international stage, so he went to Ghana. On that point, he and Garvey actually agreed. He was saying that when you have a nation that evolves around white supremacy, predatory capitalism, militarism of its empire, and sexism in its households and civil society, then the basic message to Black people is that Black freedom is a pipedream. Black history is a curse. Black hope is a joke. Defer and adjust. But, we come from a tradition that says white supremacy is a lie, but it's very much alive.

So, when you lay out these facts, you can see the sheer pathology of white supremacy. You can't even appeal to people's material interest. So what do we then do? Well… we gotta tell the truth. We gotta bear witness. We gotta build our institutions. We have to hold on to one another. We have to create whatever multiracial coalitions we can for people who are willing to be part of a coalition in which white supremacy is still fundamental. You not gon' form a coalition with white supremacy pushed to the side. Because then you don't have a coalition. In that case, you have interest group articulation to see the ways in which some kind of interest based calculus as opposed to a principled coalition can take place. But the history of Black folk, ever since we got off the boat, has had a reflective and toxic character. This is why we have to keep fighting, keep writing, keep laughing, keep singing, keep loving our children, etc. Now as a Christian, of course, we have to wear the cross. Martin said, the cross is not just symbolic. It's something you pick up, carry, and die on. If you tell the truth about white supremacy in America, you are going to get character assassination, or literal assassination coming at you. Sometimes from your own oppressed people.

LK

Let me share a bit of data, and hopefully this can inform your response to my next question. Very recently, the Metropolitan Planning Council here in Chicago released a major report (2017) entitled *The Cost of Segregation*. The authors of the report revealed that in Chicago, chronic, concentrated segregation costs the city over $4.5 billion per year. The report goes on to reveal how segregation adversely affects jobs, income, education, and housing throughout the city. The findings are quite toxic. Now, these are themes echoed in poor communities across the country. In your view, how should everyday people interpret and respond to these findings?

HM

Well, one way is to demand universal healthcare. One of the problems that you did not mention is stress, strain, and the ways that people attempt to cope with isolation in these communities where these problems exist. Where people have to go to school and work every day, and are forced to try to deal with these problems day in and day out. So, the pressure, tension, and stress that folks are dealing with is a major part of this problem. It's always a battle. The other thing is how do we begin to deal with long-term education and care for the incarcerated who get released back into our communities? We do not currently have the resources to do justice to that issue. It gets back always to the thing that all of us are trying to do: organize. You cannot stop or start anything without organized struggle. The only reason that [Chicago mayor] Rahm Em-manuel responded to any populist issues during our most recent election is because he had a serious challenger [Jesus 'Chuy' Gar-cia] threatening his seat. But see, this is where the money thing comes in because he [Rahm Emmanuel] reached out to his rich brother [Ari Emmanuel] out there on the west coast, came back to Chicago with a few million dollars, and started passing it out the Black community. So, money trumps a lot of this stuff. We do not have serious access to resources. That's a serious problem. Espe-cially when you have to make payroll every two weeks.

LK

Yes. The report I mentioned also offered policy recommendations. The most basic of which calls for us to dismantle segregation in the city. But, that brings up another challenge because how do peo-ple who have been perpetually privileged... I mean, when you talk about introducing equality to a privileged person, they perceive that as being oppressive. That is, they perceive it as you trying to take what they have, which would then make them uncomfortable. I'm reminded of the Irish muckraker Finley Peter Dunne who would remind journalists of their obligation to seek the truth. He'd say their job is *"to afflict the comfortable, and to comfort the afflicted."* How do you do that (i.e., dismantle the segregation) when so many peo-ple benefit from it, and may perceive any form of evening, or parity as a form of oppression?

MP

Let me just connect that to a situation we see in Chicago right now with the violence. We should not be at all surprised with what we see. The truth of the matter is, as horrific as the numbers are... seven people killed just yesterday, not too many blocks from here.

Umm... sometimes when I look at the reality, I'm surprised there's not more violence. Back around 1985, the *Chicago Tribune* put out this 22-page piece about the Chicago. I really the believe the purpose of that was to embarrass then Mayor Harold Washington, who was gearing up to run again in 1987. I think that was the purpose of it. What the piece did do was lay out all of the city's problems with crime, violence, housing, education, poverty, etc. You can take that 1985 piece and bring it up to 2017 – change the dates, change the names – and it's the exact same situation. What that tells us is that if we know what the problem is, and we're not doing anything about it, then we choose not to do anything about it.

In Chicago, we turn around what we want to turn around. We turned around the West Loop. I used to run a soup kitchen on Madison Street. It was called Skid Row in 1974-5. Now I can't afford restaurants on "Skid Row." Look at the South Loop. Million dollar homes over there now. Used to be Maxwell Street. In this city, we turn around what we choose to. So, if we look at these 13 to 15 neighborhoods (out of the 77 neighborhoods in Chicago) where the most violence is happening, you see double-digit unemployment, the highest recidivism rates, the most foreclosed and abandoned homes, underperforming and underfunded schools, abandoned lots, boarded up buildings, etc. You see neighborhoods that look like Third World countries. So, I think the earlier approach was to confine the south and west sides. That was then. Now what you have is people who ran to the suburbs coming back to the city. So now, they want to get those neighborhoods back. They want those neighborhoods. Look at South Shore. That's a golden neighborhood. Look at what's going on where they're buying up property. When I look at Bronzeville, a great Black metropolis... when I ride down the street... I actually stopped a month or two ago when I saw these two young white women walking down the street. I stopped them and asked *"Do you live here?"* And one of the women said *"Yeah, I live right over here."* So, I'm watching gentrification take place. I'm looking at Kennedy-King College [on the south side of Chicago]. When they start building and bringing in a Whole Foods and a Chipotle and a Starbucks... then you better look out. Something's getting ready to happen there. So, when we look at these neighborhoods that have been abandoned and neglected, they wanted to confine them, but now they want those neighborhoods. And at some point, I believe the approach might be to let the crime, poverty, and abandonment all continue so people can... I mean right now, we're seeing this great, fluid movement of people migrate out of Chicago. In fact, during the last two years, I have lost five families from my school. Some are now leaving because they're sending their sons to another part of the country because they're afraid of their child living in Chicago. In some cases, entire families are leaving.

So, if the situation becomes bad enough to force people out, then you'll see developers come in and raise prices to get rid of whomever else they want, then they'll take back these neighborhoods. This is how they provide housing and space for folks desiring to move back to the city. I sat in a meeting with a pretty well know African American pastor from the south side who said *"I don't want low-income housing in my area. I want market-value because I want to bring the right folks in my area."* I got so angry. I say, *"Are you serious?"* So, I think what we've seen happen here is that this abandonment and neglect has been on purpose. Years upon years upon years. I had a cop, a Chicago policeman say to me that if rival gang members kill one another, then the city and the state save money. There's no more LINK card, no more insurance, less problems in the street. In short, we save money on them. But when they get them in prison, they make money off them. He said you don't understand, Pfleger, *"it's a win-win."* This is a cop. He's speaking openly and bluntly with me. Essentially he's saying that violence is a business. Poverty is a business. Nothing that we're seeing is by accident, it's by design.

LK

Let me turn this question over to Father Pfleger. A recent *New Yorker* article about you from last year. I believe it was from October 2016. The article described a tension that you felt that you experienced in wanting to be close to the mayor of Chicago while also needing to remain a critic of the mayor. And so, you've done more than most in the fight for economic and social justice. The report I mentioned earlier from the Metropolitan Council about Chicago segregation did offer suggestions for desegregating Chicago and the report's authors offered that as the remedy. In your view, is that a realistic proposal? Especially if the privileged view equality as oppressive to them?

MP

Well I have two responses. The first response involves the tension spot with the mayor that you mentioned. With regard to the mayor (or even the governor or the president), I refuse to just dismiss them, and not make them responsible for who they're supposed to be as elected leaders. So, I'm never gonna say that I'll have nothing to do with them, or I that I don't respect their office. Now, I may not like what they're doing in their office, and I will hope they won't be there long, but for right now… they're here. And therefore, they have a responsibility to the community. I want to be able to maintain a conversation. [Former] Mayor Daley said something to me once that I've always loved. I've since said it to Mayor Emanuel, and to others. Mayor Daley once said to me *"When you come to my office, Mike, I never know if you're coming to ask me to go to lunch, or if you're coming to demonstrate."* And I said, *"That's the perfect relationship that I want. I'll stand with you when you're doing something right. But I'm going to fight you when you're doing something wrong."* So, that's how I try to keep that relationship working while they're in power. Um... but... in terms of the segregation thing in Chicago... umm... obviously... well... I'm channeling Dr. King. That is to say, I believe in people living together and working together. But like Haki talked about when he was holding the hand of a nun during that protest march in Marquette Park... King had a magnificent way of bringing together people from all walks of life. He used to always describe it as bringing them to the moral center; bringing them to our side in the moral center. He had a tremendous ability to do that. To me, what's been so difficult is that when you're trying to create an open, diverse, and integrated community, it almost always means lose your community.

The reality of it are is that you most always lose it. I agree with King that until we get to the hearts of people, we cannot get people to respect each other as neighbors, and as brothers and sisters in the street or around the the block. So, I still think, as I mentioned earlier, that even though the report [on segregation] made mention of the money lost because of segregation... it's striking that they would rather lose that money than integrate a neighborhood. They don't mind losing the money. Because they've also learned to take back neighborhoods, and to repopulate them. But for me, being faithful to Jesus (whom I try to sever), but also being faithful to King who influenced me... it's clear that we always have to try to work toward true brotherhood and sisterhood. We can never lose that hope. I just think that we always have to move toward it with a very critical eye. Because there's always an agenda. And, as Dr. West and Dr. Madhubuti mentioned earlier, you have so many folks in the community who will sell out in order to assimilate and fit into the very structure that's destroying us. So you gotta watch the government, the guy down the street, the developer, etc. There's so much at stake. So we always have to move into that source of integration. Dr. King once warned that we may be integrating into a burning house. So that's not what we want. We want to integrate into true equality, fairness, equity, and justice. And Lord knows that's hard.

Conversation Part Three

Kicking Rocks in the
Get-Over Culture

When the rather unique opportunity presented itself to have a conversation/dialogue with two of the most committed Christian activists and political thinkers in the nation, even I saw the "light." Having been involved in political/cultural struggle, particularly Black struggle, at the national and international levels all of my adult life, I have been able to witness serious workers as well as serious traitors among us. I have seen how Christianity has been pimped and used effectively as a means to personally enrich some at the expense of the needy and ignorant among most people. Therefore, I viewed the intimate, unscripted, open-ended back-and-forth with Dr. Cornel West and Reverend Father Michael Pfleger as a gift during these perilous times.

Having been raised a Christian, like most Black people in the United States, I have suffered dearly from those men who profess to be the critical interpreter, deliverer, and on earth messenger of the word of Christ. My paternal grandfather was a store front Baptist preacher and was as serious as a first love about his calling, mission, and responsibility. He indeed was a good man, a family man who worked diligently in the secular world six days a week to provide love, food, clothing, housing, education and his uncontested Christian-view of the world to his family, extended family and congregation.

However, I as a boy and teenager, witnessed in horror how a good number of men of Christ, men of Islam, Hinduism, and other—at that time spiritual paths unknown to me—used and abused sexually and "religiously" the dearest person to me, my mother. My mother, in her early twenties, was one of the most beautiful women—physically and spiritually—in my young world. Often, when she would take me and my sister on weekend walks her beauty would not only stop men in cars (of all colors), offering us a ride, her wonderment would stop buses. Upon arrival in Detroit from Little Rock, Arkansas in the early 1940s, (I am currently 75 years of age) we immediately, on the first Sunday there, sought out a church home. Based upon several recommendations, we arrived at one of the largest Black churches in Detroit and sat very close to the front, where we could see and hear the ministers message. That began our unexpected downfall.

The "Right" Reverend Doctor could not take his eyes off of my mother as he stumbled through his sermon. After the service, as we exited the church, he greeted us with a big smile and grabbed my mother's right hand and whispered in her ear while putting a piece of paper in her hand. By the end of the week, we had moved into a basement apartment in one of his buildings. She, to the outside world was the new janitor of the building. Within the second week, I had learned the real reason for our "good" fortune. The reverend would visit my mother for sex twice a week. Unknown, I'm sure to his wife and parishioners. This was my mother's introduction to a life of sexual survival. Yet, the action that really challenged my young mind was the minister telling her and us to never come back to his church. My question to my mother was, why? There was no answer from her. This started for me, a long and difficult life of questioning my own connection to Christianity and all religions. I viewed his behavior—even at a young age—as cruel, un-Christian and a betrayal to his "calling."

My answer along with a lifetime of study is that I must be of service to our community and daily fight for that which is good, just, right, correct and necessary with a sense of integrity. Yes, it was also on that day that I left the church and watched the deadly decline of my mother. By the time she was 34, she was dead and my sister and I were on our own.

Both Dr. West, and Reverend Pfleger and I are good friends. I have two other friends of the cloth, Bishop Frank M. Reid of Baltimore and now retired Reverend Dr. Jeremiah Wright of Chicago. They have not renewed my faith, but their Christian commitment to our people cannot be denied or made small. Each of them remain culturally Black and my respect for them remain unshaken. They unlike most people in the United States and in the Black community in particular, understand the critical importance of Black history, heritage, culture, and religion. It is clear to me after over fifty-years as a poet, writer, educator and builder of independent Black institutions that the most powerful, richest and successful Black business in our community is the Black Church. With its non-profit status, the Black Church's ability to raise money and to use such funds without "controls" has allowed it to effectively create and often use "religion" as the get-over spiritual road to major wealth and institutional status.

I see as a major problem facing the majority of the nation's people and in particular Black people is ignorance. Most of us do what we've been taught to do and seldom do we reach early enlightenment as a result of poor education. There is a deep unknowing in most of us. This is especially true in all of the life giving and life saving areas of wellness: food production, consumption and the importance of plant-based nutrition, economics (gangster capitalism in all of its many disguises and the creation of fair labor laws), politics and civics (the absolute necessity of true democracy), education (free schooling preK-Graduate School), law, taxes and prison industrial complex (understanding how the powerful use law, tax and prison policy against the powerless), social (how people and families relate), creativity (the unusual power of art: music, literature, language, dance, drama, film, photography, architecture, etc.), science (especially environmental science), ethics and morality, gender and sexuality (diversity and inclusion), health (physical, mental and spiritual), war (why ongoing wars are fought by the poor, the absolute strength of the armament industry and why it will never be outsourced), peace (the basis for clean food, clean water, clean people, clean ideas), world spirituality and finally, race (questioning and accepting one's ethnicity not only in America, but internationally, with an in-depth understanding of the danger of global white supremacy and nationalism). In this highly debased, corrupt, stolen political and economic rulership we are still kicking rocks, but we are not alone. There is always a way with men like West, Pfleger, Kazembe and millions of other women and men, especially, Heather Heyer and Sandra Bland, two recent martyrs.

Many thanks to Dr. Lasana Kazembe for his awesome work in pulling together this meeting and the creation of this book.

Dr. Haki Madhubuti
September 8, 2017

Reflections on Radical Love and Commitment

LK

This is a perfect segue for Brother West. Earlier this morning before we got started, we were reflecting on the great James Baldwin. In one of your recent tweets, you wrote *"Baldwin's painful self-examination led to a collective action and a focus on social movements."* In light of the recent documentary (*I Am Not Your Negro*), do you feel that message is getting through? By that, I mean the message in Baldwin's message about collective action. We shall overcome versus the 'Me Phi Me' age in which we find ourselves. Do you think that's getting through, particularly to the younger people? In other words, how are we supposed to engage Baldwin's ideas concerning the power of collective action of the people, while resisting the allure of a spectatorial, non-critical stance?

CW

Well, I do want to salute Raoul Peck's film. He's a Haitian brother. I think he did a wonderful job. *Remember This House* is the book that Baldwin was going to write about the deaths of his very, very good friends and comrades Medgar Evers, Malcolm X, and Martin Luther King, Jr. Baldwin has a fundamental commitment to what he calls 'paying his dues.' This is part of my struggle with my dear Brother Coates. Ta-Nehisi Coates. Toni Morrison called him the new James Baldwin. But I say that's not a compliment. That's not

an appropriate thing to say. Coates is a talented journalist. Baldwin
is a great writer. Baldwin always believe in paying his dues in terms
of acknowledging that there's no such thing as white supremacy
without resistance. There's no such thing as white supremacy without fight back. There's never been one moment of white supremacy
in the world without Black folks fighting back. And so, Baldwin
paying his dues means he's got to be in solidarity alongside the fight
back. And of course, it began in the late 1950s mainly with the children. "Somebody paid the dues for me, I gotta pay the dues back."
That's Baldwin. So he was a great artist, a great writer, a master of
his craft. But he was part of the fight back. He was a part of what
it means to really bear witness. That's what Baldwin was. He was
a witness bearer at the deepest level. So the legacy of James Baldwin is a really a legacy of mastery of craft. It's a legacy of being
true to himself. Brother Haki and I were talking about the times
he's sat with James Baldwin. Many, many hours. At the house of
Gwendolyn Brooks. He got to see what Baldwin was like just as a
human being. I met Baldwin at a club in Harlem, but I never spent
that kind of quality time with him like Brother Haki. But that's
what I had in mind regarding the legacy of Baldwin. And I do believe that legacy is being embraced much more by the younger generation than the older generation. The Black Lives Matter
Movement. And sometimes I just consider the sheer number of
young Black people who are in the movement today, and who are
on fire for justice, but remain anonymous. They are responding to
Baldwin's legacy. I think much more than my generation.

HM
You know that may be true. But it's more of a… They haven't read
Baldwin. That's what I'm trying to say. In my generation, we read
Baldwin. We actually studied Baldwin.

LK

In your generation, they *read*.

[LAUGHTER]

HM

Touché [LAUGHTER]. But I think that's the primary difference. We have to get to the young folks in Black Lives Matter. And I'm speaking for Third World Press Foundation. We'll send them to books for free. We'll send them the destruction of black civilization. Will send them black man obsolete single and dangerous. Whatever they want free. As a donation. And we can even come into their space and dialogue with him about the text. But they have to have this historical consciousness in terms of not making the mistakes our generation made. And it's always much easier to believe than to think. Thinking requires introspection. It requires additional knowledge. Not only from one's own culture but from other cultures. I can dialogue with [former Mayor] Daley, too, and he knew I didn't like him. And I even ended up writing a poem about him. Primarily because he saved the libraries in the city. And I told him that. I said that's the only reason I care about you is because you saved the libraries. And that was his last good act. One of his worst acts was selling these damn parking meters. And he got cheated on that. But to get back to Baldwin he was such an extraordinary person. He was just like Hoyt Fuller. Fuller was one of the first genuine black intellectuals I had met who had actually traveled the world. Before he started editing *Negro Digest/Black World* magazine. And Hoyt was gay. And it didn't stop him. One of the reasons Hoyt got fired from black world magazine is because he allowed the Palestinian side of the struggle in the Middle East to be told in the magazine. I wrote about it and claiming earth. And

John Johnson told him he couldn't do that. And Hoyt said if I'm going to have this kind of freedom around editing the magazine I'm going to do what I want to do. So he was fired.

CW
And that was 19-

HM
It was 1976.

CW
Mid-seventies that's what I was going to say. Right.

HM
And so we set up a picket line outside the new headquarters on Michigan Avenue. I was the spokesperson for that. John Henrik Clarke came in. So you know it was a big thing. And when we got upstairs to the conference room I asked Johnson why hear fired Fuller. And he told the truth. The Jewish community came after me and told me that if I want to continue to pay for this building, if I want to have advertising in my magazine then I had better fire Fuller. And that's why Hoyt had to leave. Baldwin had that same kind of integrity and spirit. Remember Baldwin became known by publishing in *Commentary* [magazine]. Yet, even though he had that kind of connection to certain elements within the Jewish community he did not allow that to stop him from criticizing that which was incorrect. And I met him over there on 2428 South Everett Avenue. Sitting on Gwendolyn Brooks's couch. We were arguing back and forth about Vietnam. But it was all in good spirit. And I think I mentioned to you earlier I did the last interview with James Baldwin at Cornell University. It was around literature and other areas.

He loved King and Malcolm. I didn't know his association with Medger Evers until after I saw the film. His is work is timeless. You can go back and read any of his essays and even his novels to understand where we are right now.

MP

But you know Haki, something else which is so key is the importance of building capacity. Those protesters they couldn't come to Johnson to say that if there wasn't capacity. And when look at so much black media today we see that they're owned and therefore their controlled. John Rodgers always talks about the black millionaires in Chicago like Johnson Products. All of these black millionaires that existed but are not there now.

HM

No they're not there.

MP

So we've lost that. So until there is capacity there's always a danger of being controlled.

LK

Just a side note all of those old editions of Negro digest black world magazine have been digitized by Google. You can actually go back now and look at them you can see these articles in the magazine that are critical of the Israeli occupation. And then you see that it stopped.

HM

Right. That's why I respected Fuller so much. After he got fired he is gotten a job at Cornell. He had moved back to Atlanta and he would fly from Atlanta to Cornell every week I guess. At least two or three times a month. We it started this magazine called first world.

CW
I remember the first world.

HM
At the time Hoyt died, he had been delivering copies of first world magazine to the post office. He just dropped dead. He had a heart condition. I think he was in his middle 50s.

LK
Let's make a quick transition. We spoke about this over lunch. I teach Africana Studies, and at the beginning of my classes I play music as the students are coming in and getting seated. And when I asked them to rise and bring the papers up I have music playing. So while they're walking in and waiting for class to start, I'm playing Albert Ayler and Alice Coltrane. The Stylistics and Lionel Hampton. I'm playing Muddy Waters, Blind Lemon Jefferson, and Ella Fitzgerald, you know? I'm dropping scat, bebop, blues. All that stuff plus conscious hip-hop.

CW
[LAUGHTER] I need to take your class!

MP
Me too!

LK
At 7:30am! They're listening to Dizzy Gillespie blowing!

CW
Ooo-wee!!

LK
When I look at their faces and when I talk to them about that music they just go silent. Some of them you know they're listening to Ella performing *One Note Samba* and they're wondering what she's doing. *Does she have something stuck in her throat? What is she saying?* You know? And, of course, they've never heard of any of these people. Which is tragic. As an educator, I view this as an opportunity. Their lack of knowledge of such things and people who are really not that far away from us that's been described as a form of cultural illiteracy. What are your thoughts about this generation's disconnection from its own history and traditions? Which for us has always found its deepest expression via song, dance, and drum. What's the danger when the current generation loses touch with the former generation and its traditions?

HM
They lose the language. They're not even able to communicate with each other and have a common source of knowledge. That's very sad. We all do what we've been taught to do. And if you've not been taught then your peers become your teachers and they don't know too much of anything anyway. And this is where this whole 'me' generation comes from. Most of us out here doing this work were brought up in an 'our' generation. There is a profound difference between being an individual and individualism. As artists, we have to be individuals but we have to understand that we cannot be individualistic. Especially if we're trying to move our art to another level. We should always be dealing with the community. At the same time, you have to have mentors. And when I say mentors

I'm not talking about drive-by mentors. You have to have someone who's going to spend quality time with you doing things that are meaningful. Essentially that's what we do here. So I have all of these cultural sons and daughters. We have to have these family connections with people especially young people because they needed the most. I knew I needed it when I came up. The only thing that saved me was art. So music becomes that connection. But these days the musicians are copying the copiers. So therefore they don't go back to the original sources you mentioned earlier. And they do not have that kind of bonding tradition that allows them to build on the Louis Armstrongs the Miles Davises and so forth.

LK

Brother West there is as you know a growing and disturbing trend of anti-intellectualism and elitism in American culture. I think this is a related question. In our time we're witnessing the dismissal of science, the arts, humanities etc. They're being replaced by entertainment and self-righteousness and a widening narcissism. The Roman poet Juvenal used the term *"bread and circuses"* to critique the selfishness of the common people in their neglect of deeper concerns. The late philosopher Sheldon Wolin described this tendency as *"inverted totalitarianism"* or a form of self-oppression. What, in your opinion, needs to be summoned in order to counter that, particularly among a human collective that is, in your own words *"world weary?"*

CW

Well for one thing, the pervasive worship of mediocrity that's inseparable from a captivity to American idolatry generates a culture that is superficial and where ignorance itself can parade as some-

68

thing appealing and attractive rather than as something to be pushed aside in the name of wisdom. So the only thing we have left is the call for revolution. There has to be a revolution in our priorities. That's the way Martin talked about it. There has to be a revolution in our psyches and our souls and in our communities that Malcolm reminded us of. And by revolution what we're talking about is not some kind of sophomoric fight with instrumentalities of violence. Instead what we're talking about our fundamental forms of awakening. And they are political and spiritual. And they do produce a revolution in society in terms of fundamental transformation of the society. The transfer of power and wealth and so on. Those are the consequences.

But the pillars are massive forms of awakening that shatters not just ignorance, but also shatters callousness. It shatters indifference towards the week and the vulnerable. It shatters cowardice. We have to make fortitude and moral courage hip. It has to become something that people fall in love with. One of the great joys of my own life is to be able to sit at a table with brothers like these two. That is a joy. It's not just a pleasure. Most of American culture is a joyless quest for pleasure. Young folks don't have too many joys but they have a whole lot pleasures. All they last for and so forth. They're still empty after they orgasm. They're still empty after the bottle is empty. And so how do we bring back Joy? Joy is a fruit of an awakening that is tied to labor and struggle and rooted in conviction and commitment. And that is something that never goes out of style. It's like love. Love never goes out of style. It's timeless. Which is to say it's always timely. That's what timelessness means. We're not talking about eternity but we mean it's relevant to every time. Every context. And justice is the same way.

So when we look at the mediocrity and the dumbing down, the countervailing forces, the counterculture the counterhegemonic ways of life always result from fundamental transformation tied to awakening. Education at its deepest level is mature awakening to further fortify you in a struggle against evil. That's why solidarity is so very important.

LK

Let me address this next question to Father Pfleger. After that everyone please feel free share your thoughts. We've talked a lot in this conversation about values, we talked about integrity, we talked a lot about a lot of the fundamental things that human beings need to muster. What are some of the core values and ideas that you bring to your own work? And talk to me about who have been the inspirational people in your life whose examples continue to influence you as you approach your work? And, if I can invoke the spirit of our communist friends, can you please name names?

[LAUGHTER]

MP

I think some of the core values are reflected in the we that Haki talks about. Never live for the I but live for the we. Faith unquestionably. You have to recognize that there something bigger than you. I think the value of love whether it's at the cross or at the Lorraine Motel Love is still more powerful. Love has to be the thread that weaves together whatever we do. Truth. Being authentic. And what Haki talked about earlier in terms of commitment. There's a lot of pop-up activists these days. The question is will they be there tomorrow? Will they be there next month?

CW

Will they be there next week?

MP

Exactly. If you're not in there for the long term then don't get in there. And so do engage our work by witness, by conversation, and by legacy. I'm sitting with two of them. I laughed often with them about certain things. Back when he was Don L. Lee, his *Book of Life* took me through very difficult times in college. That book is so worn out on my shelf to this very day. Because that book did so much for me. So for me to go from reading his book to later calling him a friend and interacting with him throughout these years is priceless. Brother West. To see his willingness to stay true to himself. Let me say something else before I get into anymore names. One of the things that folks like this and Belafonte and Farrakhan and Jeremiah Wright have witnessed to me is if you're going to truly be in any semblance of the word prophetic, you have to almost be an outcast to your profession. To the education and arts professions, Haki has been a voice that they cannot dumb down and a force that they cannot tamp down. He's going to continue to be the voice of conscience. He's going to continue using art to form and shape and mold enter strengthen convictions and not to entertain. Same thing with Brother West in education. How many people have we watched going into education white and black who've assimilated in and now become the overseers of education and no longer the voice of education as a tool that stimulates and stretches you and pulls you and makes demands of you. And with me in the church I've always been this fringe this thorn this problem in the side of the church. And in all honesty I think that can be very painful and difficult and not easy. And you have to mature to a point where you can be okay with that. Okay with not being appreciated or liked or valued in your field. I think you have to be okay with that. And Haki you can identify with this, we're always trying to make the next payroll. Because you are not going to have money thrown at you if you are a conscious voice. That's why so many people as Shirley Chisholm would say are bought and bossed. Unbought and unbossed is what she said we have to remain. But it's difficult. Dealing with all the other stuff and the practical stuff to: keeping the building open keeping the lights on, keeping the heat on keeping the school going. It's difficult. It's painful. And being an outcast at same time. Having people throw daggers at you publicly and nationally. It's painful. So I need people like Cornel West, like Haki and Belafonte, and Farrakhan, and Jeremiah Wright who took the daggers. But I can look at myself in the mirror. Truth and integrity are more important than popularity and appreciation. So those are folks that I look to and say wow they're doing it.

One of the comment about the young people that is important to me is that I love their zeal and their outrage. However, with some of them I'm frightened by their disconnection from history and the disconnection from their own folks. Take for instance the brothers I deal with on 79th St. and 69th St. When I try to get them to come to an event, they don't give an 'f' about me. Those black kids down there they won't come here. And they're right. So here are the black lives matters individuals struggling to keep from being shot or killed or being throwaways. So we have to connect them to the people. You have to connect to all of your brothers and sisters not just the high-profile ones who may have been shot by the cops on the corner. But the ones you can't go to school or can't get a job or who are living on the street. In his sermon on the four little girls who were bombed, Dr. King said if we want to arrest the bomber, we have to arrest the system that produced the bomber. Unless we know history then we'll get caught up with [Jason] van Dyke going to prison. But if we don't know history we're not going to change the system that produced van Dyke. So we got to do both. We to point to what's wrong but also at what created the wrong. What created van Dyke and all of the other van Dykes that might be under the radar? So I look at the people who see that historical perspective who are fighting and relevant today and have that appreciation and that knowledge and that honoring of history. And they're free. We may be in debt, but we're free.

[LAUGHTER]

HM
That's true. [LAUGHS]

CW
And you all have the respect; the genuine respect of so many others.

HM
Well as we move toward ending this very powerful and beautiful conversation, I think there are unconditionals in the context of our lives. Especially for those of us who've been around for a while. I write about this briefly in *Taking Bullets*. The first one is unconditional love. You can't have unconditional love for others unless you have unconditional love for yourself. And what happens is that unconditional love solves one of the major problems in our community which is fear. When 9/11 happened it didn't bother me that much except for the people being killed. Innocent people die. But 9/11 didn't frighten me. Because that was just blowback. If you understand history then you knew what was happening. But the

Bushes and the Cheneys used it to start a war. They used ignorance. So what part of our job is to solve that problem. How do I we get the truth without? Especially now in the era of alt truth and falls narrative. So this whole unconditional love starts with an understanding that it goes beyond us to the brothers and sisters that we deal with. The other would be unconditional courage. We have to have that everyday. The ability to question authority. Unconditional search. That's why knowledge is so important. Especially a knowledge based culture. And unconditional will. Meaning what is it that get you up each and every day. Why do I exercise six and seven days out of the week? The key point is we have to stay in shape and to be ready for the battle. I thought at 75, I'd be able to slow down a little bit. [LAUGHS]

[LAUGHTER]

MP
You thought.

HRM
It's not going happen.

CW
He [Haki] got up at four o'clock this morning to travel from South Carolina. With a smile on his face.

HM
That's cause I saw you.

[LAUGHTER]
But the he (Cornel) comes all the way from Boston. Getting up at

maybe two or three o'clock o'clock in the morning. And this is critical... he came here on his own dime. He's never asked me for any money. The same with Mike. In fact, we published a book and we were trying to use the proceeds as a fundraiser.

LK

In His Image.

HM

Right. I tried to get all these preachers in Chicago to buy the book. So I went and talked to Mike. I'm in real trouble now [LAUGHS]. And he gave me a check for two thousand dollars.

CW

Wow! Lord have mercy.

HM

That's love. But the point is we have to recognize they were all in need of a certain level and we need to help each other. That's why you don't have any checks coming from Third World Press Foundation to Haki Madhubuti. I've never taken a salary. My wife and I have never taken a salary from the schools. Never. Because this is a service. So I don't have a problem cussing a negro out. Because it's not me is for our babies.

LK

Well this is not my last question but it's the last one I'll ask. One of you recently tweeted. I won't say who it was [pointing at Cornel West]

[LAUGHTER]

KEEPING PEACE: REFLECTIONS ON

One of you recently tweeted *"just telling the truth and having integrity is revolutionary, subversive and countercultural."* That was tweeted. Even those remotely familiar with each of you and your work understands that this typifies your work in the collective struggle that you bring to your work. Does this sentiment also conform to the legacy that you'd like to leave? What lessons, examples, themes should we the people draw from your lives and examples. What inheritance would you like to leave us with?

HM
I really don't have to worry about that because my birthday is on the same day as W.E.B. DuBois.

[LAUGHTER]

So the only thing I really worry about I just want people to say that he was good man. He was a good father. He took care of his business. Any wasn't afraid of too much. Any he read a lot.

CW
Well as long as I'm around I'll be able to say about Brother Haki that he was a great artist, and educator, and a grand lover of the people. And that he had that unconditional will and love and courage and longevity and integrity. Myself I never think you or worry about my legacy. People been lying about me so much while I've been alive I know they're gon' lie about me when I'm dead.

[LAUGHTER]

But the most important thing is while I'm here I want to be able not just to tell the truth because for me the truth is not manifest just in propositions. It's manifest in a life lived. You know Aristotle talks about the speaker. You got logos, pathos, and ethos. Logos is just your argument. With pathos we want to know is it coming from your heart and mind and soul so that people are hearing and feeling it. But the ethos is the quality of the person who speaks. That's the force behind the truth in the logos in the pathos. So if you bring all three of those together that has to do with a life well lived. You see and that's Martin Luther King. That's John Coltrane. That's Sarah Vaughan. That's what it is to be an embodiment of truth. An enactment of truth in that sense. All of us thrive and fall on our faces and bounce back every day.

HM
You know Jerry Butler sang *For Your Precious Love* (1958).

CW
Oh yeah. Lord, lord, yes.

HM
And with Mike and Cornel, that's what it is: precious love. And we have to realize that that is the key point. And what Mike is doing over there [at St. Sabina] is beyond revolutionary. It's evolutionary. And it's about tomorrow. I guess that's what I'm concerned about more than anything else. Who do you have coming behind you?

MP
I guess that what's most important to me is the young people, both those in the street and those who've gone off to college. I've tried to challenge them to be leaders. I'm not as much worried about what happens with St. Sabina. That probably sounds terrible. But

I can't control that because it's under the archdiocese umbrella so I can't pick a successor like can be done in other church organizations. So I have to focus my energy on young people to raise successors in folks that I think are free and who will remain committed and consistent and not afraid to challenge the status quo. In fact, I talked recently to one of our young adult groups. I told them that I pray that if there's anything I deposited it in you that it's uncomfortableness and being unsatisfied. That you're not trying to fit in a dying world. And that you don't become the enemy that you wants talked about. That you become comfortable with being at the center. That's what's important to me. My real hope is that I hope people will say I helped to create leaders who are rising up both in the street and in the pews. The other thing is this: I think, there's so many brothers on the street who are hurting so much and don't think anybody gives a damn about them. I just want them to know that somebody cares and somebody loves them. That matters to me. That they know that there's somebody who cares and who legitimately values them.

LK
Gentlemen, thank you. Thank you all for what can only be described as a priceless experience.

CW
What a magnificent afternoon! I want to thank you all for facilitating this. The Lord wanted us here. This has been a magnificent session.